KETO

COOKBOOK

LOSE WEIGHT AND STAY FIT WITH TASTY, LOW CARB RECIPES

[EMILY STEVENSON]

Text Copyright © [EMILY STEVENSON]

Legal & Disclaimer

The information contained in this book and its contents is not designed to replace or take the place of any form of medical or professional advice; and is not meant to replace the need for independent medical, financial, legal or other professional advice or services, as may be required. The content and information in this book has been provided for educational and entertainment purposes only.

The content and information contained in this book has been compiled from sources deemed reliable, and it is accurate to the best of the Author's knowledge, information and belief. However, the Author cannot guarantee its accuracy and validity and cannot be held liable for any errors and/or omissions. Further, changes are periodically made to this book as and when needed. Where appropriate and/or necessary, you must consult a professional (including but not limited to your doctor, attorney, financial advisor or such other professional advisor) before using any of the suggested remedies, techniques, or information in this book.

Upon using the contents and information contained in this book, you agree to hold harmless the Author from and against any damages, costs, and expenses, including any legal fees potentially resulting from the application of any of the information provided by this book. This disclaimer applies to any loss, damages or injury caused by the use and application, whether directly or indirectly, of any advice or information presented, whether for breach of contract, tort, negligence, personal injury, criminal intent, or under any other cause of action.

You agree to accept all risks of using the information presented inside this book.

You agree that by continuing to read this book, where appropriate and/or necessary, you shall consult a professional (including but not limited to your doctor, attorney, or financial advisor or such other advisor as needed) before using any of the suggested remedies, techniques, or information in this book.

TABLE OF CONTENTS

INTRODUCTION

Thank you for purchasing the book *'Keto Cookbook'*.

A keto or ketogenic diet is a low-carb, moderate protein, higher-fat diet that can help you burn fat more effectively. It has many benefits for weight loss, health, and performance, as shown in over 50 studies.

1

That's why it's recommended by a growing number of doctors and healthcare practitioners.

2

A keto diet is especially useful for losing excess body fat, reducing hunger, and improving type 2 diabetes or metabolic syndrome.

3

Here, you'll learn how to eat a keto diet based on real foods.

CONVERSION TABLES

Cooking Volume Measurement Conversion Chart				
Cup	**Fluid oz**	**Tablespoon**	**Teaspoon**	**Milliliter**
1 cup	8 oz	16 Tbsp	48 tsp	237 ml
¾ cup	6 oz	12 Tbsp	36 tsp	177 ml
$2/3$ cup	5 oz	11 Tbsp	32 tsp	158 ml
½ cup	4 oz	8 Tbsp	24 tsp	118 ml
$1/3$ cup	3 oz	5 Tbsp	16 tsp	79 ml
¼ cup	2 oz	4 Tbsp	12 tsp	59 ml
$1/8$ cup	1 oz	2 Tbsp	6 tsp	30 ml
$1/16$ cup	.5 oz	1 Tbsp	3 tsp	15 ml

Temperature Conversions

Fahrenheit	Celsius	Gas Mark	Description
225	107	1/4	Very Low
250	121	1/2	Very Low
275	135	1	Low
300	149	2	Low
325	163	3	Moderate
350	177	4	Moderate
375	190	5	Moderately Hot
400	204	6	Moderately Hot
425	218	7	Hot
450	238	8	Hot
475	246	9	Very Hot

Pounds to Kilograms conversion table

Pounds (lb)	Kilograms (kg)	Kilograms+Grams (kg+g)
1 lb	0.454 kg	0 kg 454 g
2 lb	0.907 kg	0 kg 907 g
3 lb	1.361 kg	1 kg 361 g
4 lb	1.814 kg	1 kg 814 g

KETO BREAKFAST RECIPES

1. Pumpkin Spice Waffles

Prep.Time: 10 min - Cooking Time: 20 minutes -
Servings: 2

Ingredients:

- 4 large eggs, separated into whites and yolks
- 3 tablespoons coconut flour
- 3 tablespoons powdered erythritol
- 1 ¼ teaspoon baking powder
- 1 teaspoon vanilla extract
- ½ teaspoon ground cinnamon
- ¼ teaspoon ground nutmeg
- Pinch ground cloves
- ½ cup pumpkin puree

Directions:

1. Separate the eggs into two different mixing bowls.
2. Whip the egg whites until stiff peaks form then set aside.
3. Whisk the egg yolks with the coconut flour, erythritol, baking powder, vanilla, cinnamon, nutmeg, and cloves in the other bowl.
4. Add the pumpkin puree, whisking until combined, then gently fold in the egg whites.
5. Preheat the waffle iron and grease with cooking spray.
6. Spoon about ½ cup of batter into the iron.
7. Cook the waffle according to the manufacturer's instructions.
8. Remove the waffle to a plate and repeat with the remaining batter

Nutrition: calories 265 – Fat 13.5 - Fiber 10 – Carbs 20 - Protein 16

2. Lemon Flaxseed Muffins

Prep.Time: 10 min - Cooking Time: 20 min - Servings: 12

Ingredients:

- ¾ cups almond flour
- ¼ cup ground flaxseed
- ¼ cup powdered erythritol
- 1 teaspoon baking powder
- ⅛ teaspoon salt
- ¼ cup canned coconut milk
- ¼ cup coconut oil, melted
- ¼ cup fresh lemon juice
- 3 large eggs
- 2 tablespoons grated lemon peel

Directions:

1. Preheat the oven to 350°F and line a muffin pan with paper liners.
2. Whisk the almond flour together with the ground flaxseed, erythritol, baking powder, and salt in a mixing bowl.
3. In a separate bowl, whisk together the coconut milk, coconut oil, lemon juice, and eggs.
4. Stir the wet ingredients into the dry until just combined.
5. Fold in the grated lemon peel.
6. Spoon the batter into the prepared pan and bake for 18 to 20 minutes until a knife inserted in the center comes out clean.
7. Cool the muffins in the pan for 5 minutes, then turn out onto a wire cooling rack.

Nutrition: calories 120 – Fat 11 - Fiber 1.5 – Carbs 3 - Protein 3.5

3. Keto Cream Cheese Pancakes

Prep.Time: 5 min - Cooking Time: 5 min - Servings: 8-10

Ingredients:

- 4 eggs
- 4 oz. cream cheese, softened
- 1 tbsp. sugar substitute
- 2 tsp. vanilla extract
- 4 tbsp. coconut flour
- 1½ tsp. baking powder
- Almond milk as needed

Directions:

1. Combine the eggs, cream cheese, sugar substitute, and vanilla with a blender or mixer.
2. Add the coconut flour and baking powder. Combine well. If the batter thickens after a few minutes, add a little almond milk to thin it.
3. Heat the electric griddle to 325°F. Pour the batter in 5-inch circles.
4. Wait for the surface to bubble, and then flip. Cook for 2-4 minutes longer, or until browned.
5. Serve with the toppings of your choice, or use for sandwiches.

Nutrition: calories 100 – Fat 8– Carbs 3.5 - Protein 5

4.Yummy Avocado And Salmon Breakfast Boats

Prep.Time: 5 min - Cooking Time: 25 min - Servings: 1

Ingredients:

- 1 avocado
- 1 oz. fresh goat cheese
- 2 oz. smoked salmon
- 2 tbsp. lemon juice
- 2 tbsp. of organic extra virgin olive oil
- A dash of sea salt

Directions:

1. Cut the avocado in half, removing the stone.
2. Mix the rest of the ingredients – the salmon, goat cheese, oil, lemon juice, and salt - in a food processor until they have a creamy consistency, and place the mixture inside the avocado

Nutrition: calories 520 – Fat 45 - Carbs 5 - Protein 20

5. Spinach Parmesan Egg Scramble

Prep.Time: 10 min - Cooking Time: 5 min - Servings: 4

Ingredients:

- 1 tbsp. ground cinnamon
- 4 tbsp. butter
- 1 cup milk
- 5 large eggs
- 1/4 cup sugar, confectioner
- 12 slices Texas toast
- 1 tsp. vanilla extract

Directions:

1. In a hot saucepan, liquefy the butter completely.
2. Meanwhile, cut the bread into 3 separate pieces.
3. Using a glass dish, blend the vanilla extract, melted butter, milk, and eggs thoroughly.
4. In an additional glass dish, combine the sugar and ground cinnamon.
5. Dunk each slice of bread into the wet mixture and cover with the sugar mixture completely.
6. Transfer to a dish and blend the maple syrup and brown sugar.
7. Move to the air fryer basket and fry for approximately 8 minutes while setting at 350°F.
8. Remove the sticks from the air fryer and wait for approximately 5 minutes before serving.

6. Tomato and Bacon Breakfast

Prep.Time: 25 min - Servings: 1

Ingredients:

- 3 oz aged cheddar (Tilamook)
- 1 large pastured egg
- 2 slices pastured, sugar free bacon
- 2 sprigs cilantro Handful of arugula
- 1 tsp. ghee
- Pinch of salt
- Pinch of pepper
- Pinch of turmeric

Directions:

1. Cook bacon first, you can pan fry it or pop it in the oven at 350F until crispy. Set aside.
2. Shred your cheese with a cheese grater.
3. Heat skillet on medium high heat. Once it's come to temperature add the ghee into the skillet.
4. Sprinkle the cheese into the skillet in a circle
5. It will begin to melt almost instantly. Once all of the cheese is melted and bubbling, crack the egg into the center of your cheese circle. Sprinkle the yolk with salt, pepper and turmeric.

6. Cook here for 2 minutes until the egg begins to become opaque and the cheese begins to brown.
7. Cover with a tight fitting lid and lower the heat. Cook covered for 2 minutes.
8. Remove from heat, the egg should be fully cooked and the cheese crispy.
9. Carefully slide your cheese egg onto a cutting board or dish. Use two bowls or cups, or even the cheese grater to hold up the sides of the sheet taco so that as the shell cools and hardens the sides stay up.
10. Add in your bacon, arugula and cilantro.

7. Keto Lemon Muffins With Poppy Seeds

Prep.Time: 15 min - Cooking Time: 20 min –
Servings:12

Ingredients:

- ¾ cup almond flour
- ⅓ cup Erythritol
- ¼ cup Flaxseed meal
- 1 tbsp. baking powder
- 2 tbsp. poppy seeds
- ¼ cup Butter, melted
- 3 eggs
- ¼ cup Heavy cream
- 3 tbsp. lemon juice
- Lemon zest of 2 lemons
- 1 tbsp. vanilla
- 20 drops liquid sweetener

Directions:

1. Preheat the oven to 345°F.
2. Meanwhile, mix in a bowl the flaxseed meal, almond flour, erythritol and poppy seeds.
3. Add melted butter, and mix in the eggs and heavy cream until it reaches a smooth consistency. Add the rest of the ingredients and mix.
4. Place the batter into the muffin pan (divided into 12) and bake them for 18-20 minutes.
5. Remove from the oven and cool for approximately 10 minutes.

Nutrition: calories 130 – Fat 11.5– Carbs 1.7 - Protein 4

8. Red Chocolate Doughnuts

Prep.Time: **15 min** - Cooking Time: **20 min** - Servings: **9**

Ingredients:

- ¼ cup Erythritol
- ½ cup coconut flour
- 2 tbsp. cocoa powder
- ¼ cup coconut oil
- ½ cup coconut milk
- ½ tbsp. vanilla extract
- ¼ tsp. salt
- ¼ tsp. baking soda
- 4 eggs
- ¼ tsp. apple cider vinegar
- ¼ tsp. liquid stevia
- 1 tsp. red food coloring
- For the icing:
- ¼ cup powdered erythritol
- 4 oz. cream cheese
- 4 tbsp. butter
- 2 tbsp. heavy cream
- ½ tsp. vanilla extract
- 1 tsp. red food coloring

Directions:

1. Sift the coconut flour, cocoa powder, salt and baking soda, and mix.
2. Mix the eggs, erythritol, vanilla, coconut oil, coconut milk and red food coloring. Add them into the dry ingredients and mix again.
3. Divide the batter between the molds in the donut tray. Bake in a preheated oven at 335°F for 16-18 minutes.

4. Remove the donuts from the trays and cool for 10 minutes.
5. In a pan, heat the coconut oil to its smoking point and fry the donuts on both sides. Drain them in a paper towel.
6. Combine the butter, cream cheese, heavy cream, vanilla and powdered erythritol, beating until it has a fluffy consistency. Add the food coloring, mix again, and frost the donuts.

Nutrition: calories 150 – Fat 15 - Carbs 2 - Protein 2

9. Sausage And Bacon Bite Sized Breakfasts

Prep.Time: 10 min - Cooking Time: 30 minutes - Servings: 1

Ingredients:

- 6 slices bacon
- 6 oz. breakfast sausage
- 1 tbsp. butter
- 6 eggs
- ½ tbsp. olive oil
- ¾ stalk celery
- 2 stalks leek
- ⅛ onion
- Salt and pepper

Directions:

1. In a food processor, mix the bacon and sausage together. Place the mixture into a cupcake tray, filling each cup to the top, and making a slight indent in the top of each. Bake for 15 minutes at 375°F.
2. Dice the leeks and celery, and add them to the buttered pan. Season with salt and pepper. Sauté until the celery and leeks are fairly tender. Remove the mixture from the pan and re-use the butter to fry the eggs.
3. Take the sausage bites from oven. Drain any excess oil with a paper towel, and bake again for 10 minutes.
4. Remove the baskets and fill them with the onion-leek mixture. Set the fried egg on top and serve.

Nutrition: calories 239 – Fat 20 – Carbs 2 - Protein 15

10. Sausage Casserole With Vegetables

Prep.Time: 15 min - Cooking Time: 30 min - Servings: 6

Ingredients:

- 2 cups zucchini, diced
- ¼ cup onion, diced
- 1 lb. pork sausage
- 2 cups cabbage, shredded
- 3 eggs
- 2 tbsp. mustard
- ½ cup mayonnaise
- 1½ cups cheddar cheese, shredded
- 1 tbsp. dried ground sage
- Cayenne pepper

Directions:

1. Preheat the oven to 375°F. Grease a casserole dish and set it aside.
2. In a large skillet on a medium heat, cook the sausage and the veggies until tender.
3. Place the mixture into the casserole dish.
4. In a separate bowl, mix the eggs, mustard, mayonnaise, sage, and pepper until combined well.
5. Add the grated cheese to the egg mixture and stir for 1 minute.
6. Pour the mix over the sausage and vegetables in the casserole dish, and top with the cheese.
7. Bake the casserole for 30 minutes, or remove it when it is bubbling around the edges and the cheese on the top is melted.

Nutrition: calories 480 – Fat 42 - Carbs 5 - Protein 20

11. Cheddar And Bacon Omelets With Chives

Prep.Time: 10 min - Cooking Time: 30 min - Servings: 1

Ingredients:

- 2 slices of bacon
- 2 tbsp. bacon grease
- 2 eggs
- 2 stalks of chives
- 1 oz. cheddar cheese
- Salt and pepper

Directions:

1. Place the bacon fat in a pre-heated pan on a medium-low heat, and let it melt. Add the eggs, chives, salt and pepper. Stir lightly.
2. Add the bacon once the edges are set. Cook for 20-30 seconds more.
3. Add cheese to the omelet and fold in half. Flip over and warm through on the other side.

Nutrition: calories 460 – Fat 40– Carbs 2 - Protein 25

12. Cheddar Scrambled Eggs With Spinach

Prep.Time: 10 min - Cooking Time:10 min - Servings: 1

Ingredients:

- 4 cup fresh spinach
- 4 eggs
- ½ cup cheddar cheese
- 1 tbsp. heavy cream
- 1 tbsp. olive oil
- Salt and pepper

Directions:

1. In a bowl, mix together the eggs, heavy cream, salt and pepper.
2. Heat a large pan, and add the olive oil and spinach when the oil is heated.
3. Stir the spinach, and add the salt and pepper.
4. Once the spinach is fairly wilted, add the egg mixture and turn to medium heat.
5. When the eggs are set, add the cheese and stir slowly until it melts

Nutrition: calories 700 – Fat 58 - Carbs 5 - Protein 43

13. Healhy Vegetable Breakfast Hash

Prep.Time: 10 min - Cooking Time: 15 minutes - Servings: 1

Ingredients:

- 1 medium zucchini
- ¼ cup white onion
- 2 oz. bacon
- 1 tbsp. coconut oil
- Fresh parsley, chopped
- 1 large egg
- Salt to taste

Directions:

1. Slice the bacon, and peel and dice the onion and zucchini.
2. Sauté the onion over medium heat and add the bacon. Stir and cook until slightly browned.
3. Add the zucchini to the pan, and cook for 10-15 minutes.
4. When done, place the hash on a plate and add the chopped parsley.
5. Top with a fried egg or, for an egg-free version, avocado

Nutrition: calories 427 – Fat 35 – Carbs 7 - Protein 17

14. Salted Caramel Cereal With Pork Rinds

Prep.Time: 15 min - Cooking Time: 15 min - Servings: 1

Ingredients:

- 1 oz. pork rinds
- 2 tbsp. butter
- 1 cup vanilla coconut milk
- 2 tbsp. heavy cream
- ¼ tbsp. ground cinnamon
- 1 tbsp. erythritol

Directions:

1. In a pan on a medium heat, add the butter and stir until browned.
2. Remove and add the heavy cream and erythritol. Mix well and return to the heat. Continue heating, stirring constantly until the desired caramel color is achieved.
3. Add the pork rinds and mix them in, being careful to coat evenly.
4. Place them into a container and put in the fridge for 20-45 minutes to cool them down.

Nutrition: calories 510 – Fat 50 - Carbs 2.7 - Protein 15

15. Keto Oatmeal

Prep.Time: 10 min - Cooking Time: 15 min - Servings: 2

Ingredients:

- ¼ cup shredded coconut, unsweetened
- ⅓ cup almonds, flaked
- ¼ cup chia seeds
- ⅓ cup flaked coconut, unsweetened
- 1 tsp. unsweetened vanilla extract
- 1 cup hot water
- ½ cup coconut milk
- 2 tbsp. erythritol
- 6-8 drops stevia extract

Directions:

1. In a bowl, place the flaked and shredded coconut, almonds and chia seeds, setting aside a little bit of flaked coconut and almond.
2. Add the coconut milk, vanilla extract, stevia and combine. Add hot water and let sit for 10-15 minutes.
3. Sprinkle with flaked coconuts and almonds and top with berries (optional).

Nutrition: calories 360 – Fat 30– Carbs 5 - Protein 9.5

KETO SIDES RECIPES

1. Flaxseed Crackers

Prep.Time: 1 hour and 10 min - Servings: 3

Ingredients:

- 1 cup flaxseed meal
- 3 tbsp. olive oil
- 1/4 cup apple cider vinegar
- 1-2 tsp. water
- 1/2 tsp. sea salt

Directions:

1. In a bowl mix all of the ingredients. Mix until well combined. Let the mix sit for 20 minutes.
2. Preheat oven on 300F convection bake (or 320F bake).
3. Using a spatula transfer your flaxseed mix to a sheet of parchment paper.
4. Cover with a second sheet and flatten.
5. Use a rolling pin to continue to flatten until you have a square or shape that is about 8x8.
6. Remove the top sheet of parchment paper and move the bottom sheet with dough on it to a baking pan.
7. Pop in the oven and bake for 40-45 minutes until the center is firm, when you tap it it should feel solid.
8. Remove from the oven and let cool to room temp.
9. Transfer the parchment paper with cracker mass on it to a cutting board and with a large

kitchen knife cut into squares to break into desired shapes.

2. Healthy Chicken Salad

Prep.Time: 10 min - Servings: 4

Ingredients:

- 2 cups leftover shredded chicken breast
- 2 cups cut, steamed green beans
- 1/2 cup homemade mayo 1/2 cup chopped pecans
- 1/4 cup chopped cilantro
- 1/4 cup basil leaves
- 1/4 cup mint leaves
- 1/2 tsp. salt
- 1/2 tsp. white pepper

Directions:

1. Cut and chop your herbs and pecans.
2. Shred chicken and cut green beans.
3. In a large bowl combine all the ingredients.
4. Toss gently to mix it up.

Enjoy, store for quick, healthy meals

KETO LUNCH RECIPES

1. Keto Stromboli

Prep.Time: 15 min - Cooking Time: 20 minutes - Servings: 4

Ingredients:

- 1¼ cup shredded mozzarella cheese
- 4 tbsp. almond flour
- 3 tbsp. coconut flour
- 1 egg
- 1 tsp. Italian seasoning
- 4 oz. ham
- 4 oz. cheddar cheese
- Salt and pepper

Directions:

1. Melt the mozzarella cheese in the microwave for about minute, stirring occasionally so as not to burn it.
2. In a separate bowl, mix almond flour, coconut flour, salt, and pepper and add the melted mozzarella cheese. Mix well. Then, after letting it cool down a bit, add the eggs and combine again.
3. Place the mixture on parchment paper, laying a second layer on top. Using your hands or rolling pin, flatten it out into a rectangle.
4. Remove the top layer of paper and with a knife cut diagonal lines toward the middle of the dough. They should be cut⅓ of the way in on one side. Then, cut diagonal lines on the other side too.

5. On the top of the dough, alternate slices of ham and cheese. Then, fold one side over, and then the other, to cover the filling.
6. Place on a baking sheet and bake at 400°F for 15-20 minutes.

Nutrition: calories 305 - Fat 22 - Fiber 2 - Carbs 5- Protein 25

2. Original Nasi Lemak

Prep.Time: 15 min - Cooking Time: 15 minutes-
Servings: 2

Ingredients:

For the Chicken & Egg:
- 2 chicken thighs, boneless
- ½ tsp. curry powder
- ¼ tsp. turmeric powder
- ½ tsp. lime juice
- ½ tbsp. coconut oil
- 1 egg
- A pinch of salt

For the Nasi Lemak:
- 3 tbsp. coconut milk
- 3 slices ginger
- ½ small shallot
- 1 cup riced cauliflower
- 4 slices cucumber
- Salt

Directions:

1. Rice the cauliflower and strain the water.
2. Prepare the curry powder, turmeric powder, lemon juice and salt, and marinate the chicken thighs for an hour or two in the fridge. Remove and fry.
3. Boil the coconut milk, ginger and shallot in a saucepan. When it bubbles, incorporate the cauliflower rice and mix.
4. Serve with the marinated fried chicken and fried egg

Nutrition: calories 502 – Fat 40 - Carbs- Protein 28

3. Keto Green Salad

Prep.Time: 10 min - Servings: 1

Ingredients:

- 2 oz. mixed greens
- 3 tbsp. roasted pine nuts
- 2 tbsp. raspberry vinaigrette
- 2 tbsp. parmesan, shaved
- 2 slices bacon
- Salt and pepper

Directions:

1. Cook the bacon in a pan until crunchy and well browned. Break up into pieces, and add to the rest of the ingredients in a bowl.
2. Dress the salad with the raspberry vinaigrette.

Nutrition: calories 480 – Fat 37- Carbs 4 - Protein 17

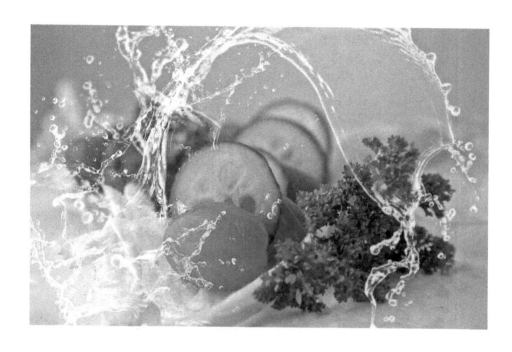

4. Tuna Bites With Avocado

Prep.Time: 10 min - Servings: 8

Ingredients:

- 10 oz. drained canned tuna
- ¼ cup mayo
- 1 avocado
- ¼ cup parmesan cheese
- ⅓ cup almond flour
- ½ tsp. garlic powder
- ¼ tsp. onion powder
- ½ cup coconut oil
- Salt and pepper

Directions:

1. In a bowl mix all the ingredients (except coconut oil). Form little balls and cover with almond flour.
2. Fry them in a pan medium heat with melted coconut oil (it has to be hot) until they seem browned on all sides.

Nutrition: calories 137 - Fat 12 - Carbs 10- Protein 6

5. Easy Egg Soup

Prep.Time: 15 min - Cooking Time: 20 minutes - Servings: 1

Ingredients:

- 1½ cups chicken broth
- ½ cube of chicken bouillon
- 1 tbsp. bacon fat
- 2 eggs
- 1 tsp. chili garlic paste

Directions:

1. In a pan on the stove on a medium-high heat, add the chicken broth, bouillon cube and bacon fat. Bring into boil and incorporate chili garlic paste and mix.
2. Whisk the eggs and add them to the chicken while stirring, then let sit for a few minutes.

Nutrition: calories 280 - Fat 25 – Carbs 2.7- Protein 13

6. Mug Cake With Jalapeno

Prep.Time: 10 min - Servings: 1

Ingredients:

- 2 tbsp. almond flour
- 1 tbsp. flaxseed meal
- 1 tbsp. butter
- 1 tbsp. cream cheese
- 1 egg
- 1 bacon slice, cooked
- ½ jalapeño pepper, sliced
- ½ tsp. baking powder
- ¼ tsp. salt

Directions:

1. Cook the bacon on a medium heat in a frying pan until crispy.
2. Mix all the ingredients in a container and pour some inside a mug. Microwave for 75 seconds on high.
3. Carefully take out the mug cake out and let cool before eating.

Nutrition: calories 430 - Fat 40- Carbs 4 - Protein 17

7. Chicken Nuggets For Keto Nuts

Prep.Time: 15 min - Cooking Time: 20 min - Servings: 4

Ingredients:

- 1 chicken breast, precooked
- ½ ounce grated parmesan
- 2 tbsp. almond flour
- ½ tsp. baking powder
- 1 egg
- 1 tbsp. water

Directions:

1. Cut the chicken breast into slices and then into bite size pieces. Set aside.
2. Combine the parmesan, almond flour, baking powder, and water. Stir.
3. Cover the chicken pieces into the batter, and then place directly into the hot oil. Remove when golden.

Nutrition: calories 165 - Fat 9 Fiber 4 - Carbs 3 - Protein 25

8. Zucchini Keto Wraps

Prep.Time: 10 min - Servings: 6

Ingredients:

- 1 zucchini
- 6 oz. soft goat's cheese
- 1 tbsp. dried mint
- 1 tsp. dried dill
- Salt and pepper
- Oil

Directions:

1. Cut off the ends of the zucchini. Slice into ⅛-inch slices and brush with oil. Grill on both sides.
2. Mix together the goat's cheese, mint and dill. Divide into 6 pieces.
3. Wrap the cheese pieces with the zucchini slices and secure with a toothpick.

Nutrition: calories 188 - Fat 14 - Fiber 8 - Carbs 4 - Protein 15

9. Keto Chicken Thighs

Prep.Time: 15 min - Cooking Time: 20 minutes - Servings: 6

Ingredients:

- 16 chicken thighs (boneless skinless)
- 2 cups water
- 8 oz. cheddar cheese, shredded
- 24 oz. spinach
- Salt and pepper
- Garlic powder

Directions:

1. Bake the chicken thighs in a covered pan with 2 cups of water at 350°F for 20 minutes. Remove and let cool.
2. Break the chicken into pieces, adding the spinach, cheese, and seasonings.

Nutrition: calories 390 - Fat 25 - Carbs 4- Protein 47

10. Grilled Cheese Sandwich

Prep.Time: 10 min - Servings: 1

Ingredients:

- 2 eggs
- 2 tbsp. almond flour
- 1 ½ tbsp. psyllium husk powder
- ½ tsp. baking powder
- 2 tbsp. soft butter
- 2 oz. cheddar cheese
- 1 tbsp. butter

Directions:

1. Mix the eggs, almond flour, psyllium husk powder, baking powder and butter to make the bun. It should be very thick. Place the mixture into a square container and let it sit to level itself. Microwave for 90 seconds.
2. When it is cooked, remove and slice in half. Place the cheese between the bun, and fry in a pan with melted butter over a medium heat.

Nutrition: calories 794 - Fat 27 - Fiber 5 - Carbs 12.5 - Protein 30

11. Chicken Salad

Prep.Time: 10 min - Cooking Time: 60 min - Servings: 6

Ingredients:

- 4 chicken breasts
- 1½ cups cream
- 4½ oz. celery
- 4 oz. green peppers
- 1 ounce green onions
- ¾ cup sugar free sweet relish
- ¾ cup mayo
- 3 eggs, hard-boiled

Directions:

1. Place the chicken in an oven-safe pan, and cover it with cream. Cook for 40-60 minutes at 350°F. When it is done, let cool. Discard the liquid.
2. Chop the celery, pepper and onions, and combine them in a bowl. Dice the chicken and add too.
3. Add chopped hardboiled eggs and mix gently.
4. Divide into 6 containers

Nutrition: calories 415 – Fat 24 - Carbs 4 - Protein 40

12. Vegetarian Curry

Prep.Time: **10 min** - Cooking Time: **60 min** -Servings: **2**

Ingredients:

- 4 tbsp. coconut oil
- ¼ onion, chopped
- 1 tsp. garlic, minced
- 1 cup broccoli florets
- Spinach
- 1 tbsp. red curry paste
- ½ cup coconut cream (or coconut milk)
- 2 tsp. soy sauce
- 1 tsp. ginger
- 2 tsp. fish sauce

Directions:

1. On a medium-high heat, add the coconut oil to a pan. Once it is hot, sauté the onions until browned. Add the garlic. Turn to a medium-low heat and add the broccoli. Stir.
2. Once the broccoli is partially cooked, add the curry paste. Let it cook for 1 minute.
3. Add the spinach. When it is cooked, add coconut cream and coconut oil. Mix and add the soy sauce, ginger and fish sauce. Simmer for approximately 10 minutes.

Nutrition: calories 395 - Fat 40 - Carbs 7 – Protein 6

13. Keto Caprese Salad

Prep.Time: 10 min - Servings: 2

Ingredients:

- 1 tomato
- 6 oz. fresh mozzarella cheese
- ¼ cup chopped fresh basil
- 3 tbsp. olive oil
- Freshly cracked black pepper
- Salt

Directions:

1. Put the fresh basil in a food processor with some oil. Blend until it forms a paste.
2. Slice the tomatoes and chop the mozzarella. On the top of each tomato, lay the mozzarella and basil paste. Season with olive oil, black pepper and salt.

Nutrition: calories 407 - Fat 38 - Carbs 3.7 - Protein 16

14. Cauliflower Rice With Chicken

Prep.Time: 15 min - Cooking Time: 30 min- Servings: 6

Ingredients:

- 4 chicken breasts
- 1 packet curry paste
- 1 cup water
- 3 tbsp. ghee
- ½ cup heavy cream
- 1 head cauliflower

Directions:

1. In a large pan, melt the ghee, add the curry, and stir. When combined, add the water, and simmer for 5 minutes.
2. Add the chicken, cover and keep cooking for 20 minutes more. When it is done, add the cream and cook for 5 additional minutes.
3. Separately, prepare the cauliflower rice: chop the head into florets and shred. Sauté in a frying pan with a little butter or olive oil, and then turn to low, covering with a lid. Let it steam for 5-8 minutes.
4. Serve along with the chicken curry.

Nutrition: calories 350 - Fat 16 - Carbs 10- Protein 40

KETO DINNER RECIPES

1. Chicken Tikka with Cauliflower Rice

Prep.Time: 10 min - Cooking Time: 6 hours- Servings: 6

Ingredients:

- 2 pounds boneless chicken thighs, chopped
- 1 cup canned coconut milk
- 1 cup heavy cream
- 3 tblsp. tomato paste
- 2 tablespoons garam masala
- 1 tblsp. fresh grated ginger
- 1 tblsp. minced garlic
- 1 tblsp. smoked paprika
- 2 tsp. onion powder
- 1 teaspoon guar gum
- 1 tablespoon butter
- 1 ½ cup riced cauliflower

Directions:

1. Spread the chicken in a slow cooker, then stir in the remaining ingredients except for the cauliflower and butter.
2. Cover and cook on low heat for 6 hours until the chicken is done and the sauce thickened.
3. Melt the butter in a saucepan over medium-high heat.
4. Add the riced cauliflower and cook for 6 to 8 minutes until tender.
5. Serve the chicken tikka with the cauliflower rice.

Nutrition: calories 485 – Fat 32 - Fiber 1.5 - Carbs 6.5- Protein 43

2. Beef and Broccoli Stir-Fry

Prep.Time: 20 min - Cooking Time: 15 min - Servings: 4

Ingredients:

- ¼ cup soy sauce
- 1 tablespoon sesame oil
- 1 teaspoon garlic chili paste
- 1 pound beef sirloin
- 2 tablespoons almond flour
- 2 tablespoons coconut oil
- 2 cups chopped broccoli florets
- 1 tablespoon grated ginger
- 3 cloves garlic, minced

Directions:

1. Whisk together the soy sauce, sesame oil, and chili paste in a small bowl.
2. Slice the beef and toss with almond flour, then place in a plastic freezer bag.
3. Pour in the sauce and toss to coat, then let rest for 20 minutes.
4. Heat the oil in a large skillet over medium-high heat.
5. Pour the beef and sauce into the skillet and cook until the beef is browned.
6. Push the beef to the sides of the skillet and add the broccoli, ginger, and garlic.
7. Sauté until the broccoli is tender-crisp, then toss it all together and serve hot.

Nutrition: calories 350 - Fat 19 - Fiber 2 - Carbs 6.5 - Protein 37.5

3. Cheddar-Stuffed Burgers with Zucchini

Prep.Time: 10 min - Cooking Time: 15 min - Servings: 4

Ingredients:

- 1 pound ground beef (80% lean)
- 2 large eggs
- ¼ cup almond flour
- 1 cup shredded cheddar cheese
- Salt and pepper
- 2 tablespoons olive oil
- 1 large zucchini, halved and sliced

Directions:

1. Combine the beef, egg, almond flour, cheese, salt, and pepper in a bowl.
2. Mix well, then shape into four even-sized patties.
3. Heat the oil in a large skillet over medium-high heat.
4. Add the burger patties and cook for 5 minutes until browned.
5. Flip the patties and add the zucchini to the skillet, tossing to coat with oil.
6. Season with salt and pepper and cook for 5 minutes, stirring the zucchini occasionally.
7. Serve the burgers with your favorite toppings and the zucchini on the side.

Nutrition: calories 470 - Fat 29.5 - Fiber 1.5 - Carbs 4.5 - Protein 47

4 Bacon-Wrapped Pork Tenderloin with Cauliflower

Prep.Time: 10 min - **Cooking Time:** 25 min - **Servings:** 4

Ingredients:

- 1 ¼ pounds boneless pork tenderloin
- Salt and pepper
- 8 slices uncooked bacon
- 1 tablespoon olive oil
- 2 cups cauliflower florets

Directions:

1. Preheat the oven to 425°F and season the pork with salt and pepper.
2. Wrap the pork in bacon and place on a foil-lined roasting pan.
3. Roast for 25 minutes until the internal temperature reaches 155°F.
4. Meanwhile, heat the oil in a skillet over medium heat.
5. Add the cauliflower and sauté until tender-crisp – about 8 to 10 minutes.
6. Turn on the broiler and place the pork under it to crisp the bacon.
7. Slice the pork to serve with the sautéed cauliflower.

Nutrition: calories 330 - Fat 18.5 - Fiber 1.5 – Carbs 3 - Protein 38

5. Lemon Chicken Kebabs with Veggies

Prep.Time: 10 min - Cooking Time: 15 min - Servings: 4

Ingredients:

- 1 pound boneless chicken thighs, cut into cubes
- ¼ cup olive oil
- 2 tblsp. lemon juice
- 1 teaspoon minced garlic
- Salt and pepper
- 1 large yellow onion, cut into 2-inch chunks
- 1 large red pepper, cut into 2-inch chunks
- 1 large green pepper, cut into 2-inch chunks

Directions:

1. Toss the chicken with the olive oil, lemon juice, garlic, salt, and pepper.
2. Slide the chicken onto skewers with the onion and peppers.
3. Preheat a grill to medium-high heat and oil the grates.
4. Grill the skewers for 2 to 3 minutes on each side until the chicken is done.

Nutrition: calories 360 - Fat 21 - Fiber 2 – Carbs 8 - Protein 34

6. Pork Hock

Prep.Time: **20 min** - Cooking Time: **4 hours** - Servings: **2**

Ingredients:

- 1 lb. pork hock
- ¼ cup rice vinegar
- ⅓ cup soy sauce
- ⅓ cup shaoxing cooking wine
- ¼ cup sweetener
- ⅓ onion
- 1 tbsp. butter
- Shiitake mushrooms
- 1 tsp. Chinese five-spice
- 1 tsp. oregano
- 2 crushed garlic cloves

Directions:

1. Fry the onions in a frying pan until semi-transparent. Meanwhile, boil the mushrooms until tender.
2. In a third pan, sear the pork hock until browned on all sides.
3. After a few minutes, add all the ingredients in a Crock-Pot and cook for 2 hours on a high heat. Stir, then cook for 2 further hours.
4. Remove the pork and bone it. Slice it and put it back to the pot so that it absorbs more flavor.
5. Serve with the vegetables.

Nutrition: calories 550 - Fat 32 - Carbs 20 - Protein 50

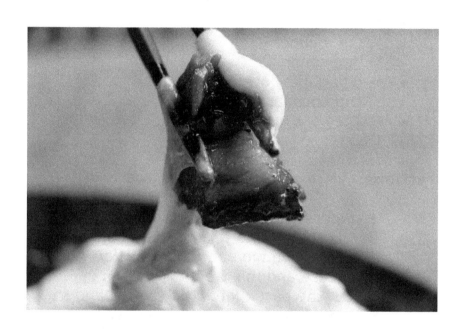

7. Meatballs With Bacon And Cheese

Prep.Time: 10 min - Cooking Time: 15 min - Servings: 5

Ingredients:

- 1½ lb. ground beef
- ¾ cup pork rinds, crushed
- ¾ tsp. salt
- ¾ tsp. pepper
- ¾ tsp. cumin
- ¾ tsp. garlic powder
- ¾ cup cheddar cheese
- 4 slices bacon
- 1 egg

Directions:

1. Process the pork rinds to make a powder.
2. Mix the ground beef, pork rinds, salt, pepper, cumin and garlic powder. Add the cheese and mix well.
3. Cut the bacon into small pieces and fry them in a hot pan until they reach the desired doneness. Let them cool. Add the bacon to the meat and combine well.
4. Form the meatballs.
5. Cook the meatballs in a pan, browning them on all sides, then cover with a lid for 10 minutes. When finished, let them sit for 5 minutes or so before enjoying. Top with the sauce of your choice.

Nutrition: calories 450 - Fat 26 - Carbs 3 - Protein 50

8. Original Keto Burger With Portobello Bun

Prep.Time: 15min - Cooking Time: 15 min - Servings: 1

Ingredients:
- 2 Portobello mushroom caps
- ½ tbsp. organic extra virgin coconut oil
- 1 garlic clove
- 1 tbsp. oregano
- 6 oz. organic grass fed beef or bison
- 1 tbsp. Dijon mustard
- 1 tsp. salt
- 1 tsp. freshly ground black pepper
- ¼ cup cheddar cheese
- Salt and pepper

Directions:
1. Clean the Portobello mushrooms, removing the stems and scraping the gills.
2. In a bowl, combine coconut oil with garlic, oregano, salt and pepper. Marinade the Portobello mushrooms in the mixture while you complete the other steps.
3. In a separate bowl, combine the ground meat, mustard, salt, black pepper and cheddar cheese. Form the patties.
4. Place the mushroom caps on a grill for 7-10 minutes. Remove and cook the burgers for 6 minutes on each side. Remove both from the heat and assemble the burger. Add preferred toppings and serve.

Nutrition: calories 730 - Fat 50 - Carbs 5- Protein 60

9. Sausage & Cabbage Skillet Melt

Prep.Time: 10 min - **Cooking Time:** 15 min - **Servings:**4

Ingredients:

- 4 spicy Italian chicken sausages
- 1½ cups green cabbage, shredded
- 1½ cups purple cabbage, shredded
- ½ cup onion, diced
- 2 tsp. coconut oil
- 2 slices Colby jack cheese
- 2 tsp. fresh cilantro, chopped

Directions:

1. Shred the cabbage (or use pre-shredded cabbage) and chop the onion.
2. Melt the coconut oil, and fry the onion and cabbage in a large skillet. Turn to medium-high and cook for 8 minutes.
3. Add the sausage, and stir to mix it into the vegetables. Cook for 8 further minutes.
4. Add the cheese on top and cover.
5. Turn off the heat and wait while the cheese melts into the vegetables.

Nutrition: calories 233 - Fat 15 - Carbs 5- Protein 20

10. Bacon Wrapped Chicken

Prep.Time: 15 min - Cooking Time: 45 min - Servings: 4

Ingredients:

- 2 skinless chicken breasts, boneless
- 2 oz. blue cheese
- 4 slices ham
- 8 slices bacon

Directions:

1. Slice the breast halves in half lengthwise.
2. Lay out 2 slices of ham, and place a line of cheese in the middle. Roll up, and place inside the chicken breast.
3. Wrap the chicken breast with 4 slices of bacon, covering the entire breast.
4. Place the breasts in an oven-proof skillet (greased with butter or coconut oil), and brown the bacon all over. Remove from the skillet and place in the oven to cook for 45 minutes at 325°F. Let sit for 10 minutes before serving.

Nutrition: calories 270 - Fat 11 - Carbs 0.5 - Protein 38

NOTE YOUR FAVORITE RECIPES

PAGE	NUMBER	RECIPE NAME

9 781802 174038